empower

publishing

Also by Lourdes Elizabeth Davis
In the *Mi Abuela* Book Series

*También por Lourdes Elizabeth Davis
en la serie de libros Mi Abuela*

Chimi

The Embroidered Bedspread
La colcha bordada

The Giant Plant
La planta gigante

and Empower Publishing

¡El Vestido!
The Dress

By

Lourdes Elizabeth Davis

empower

publishing

Empower Books
302 Ricks Drive
Winston-Salem, NC 27103

First Empower Books edition published
February, 2024
Empower Books, Feather Pen, and all production design are trademarks of Empower Publishing, used under license.

For information regarding bulk purchases of this book, digital purchase and special discounts, please contact the publisher at publish.empower.now@gmail.com

Lourdes Elizabeth Davis, Author & Illustrator
Joana Tavárez, Spanish Revisions
Dr. Linda Felker, Editor

Manufactured in the United States America
ISBN 978-1-63066-550-0

Dedicación

Toda buena dádiva y todo don perfecto desciende de lo alto, del Padre de las luces, en el cual no hay mudanza ni sombra de variación.
Santiago 1:17

Dedication

Every good gift and every perfect gift comes down from above, from the Father of lights, with whom there is no variation or shadow or variation.
James 1:17

In memory of my husband Keith Davis who motivated me to finish and publish the Mi Abuela books.

¡El Vestido!

The Dress!

Mi abuela ¡Muy inteligente era!

My grandma was very smart!

A sus doce años, me dijo mi abuela que aprendió a coser.

My grandma told me that she learned to sew when she was 12 years old.

Nadie la enseñó, pero ella aprendió.

No one taught her but she learned.

(Autodidacta le dicen a la persona que aprende sola)

This type of person is called "Self-Taught."

Ella no usaba cinta métrica, ni tampoco un patrón como la mayoría.

She did not use a measuring tape, nor did she use a pattern like most people.

Una tira de tela,
con esa media Y con las tijeras piquitos le hacía.

She used a strip from the fabric and used it to measure, and made snips with the scissors.

Aquí están los hombros,

Here the shoulders,

las mangas y este es el largo
de la espalda.

the sleeves, and the
length of the back.

Todas las medidas de la prenda tomaba:

She took measurements of all parts of the garment,

El corpiño, el busto,

The bodice, the bust,

el largo de la falda.

and the length of the skirt,

Y medía la tela y así la cortaba.

Then she measured and cut the fabric!

Su medida justa siempre terminaba.

Her measurements were always correct.

Nunca vi un cliente que se quejara.

I never heard a client complain.

Mi abuela ¡Muy inteligente era!

My grandmother was very smart!

Sucedió un día, que una clienta

It happened one day that a client

quería su vestido estrenar, pues

wanted to release her dress, because

tenía una ocasión y no quería faltar.

there was an occasion she did not want to miss.

Ella poco sabía el dilema que mi abuela tenía.

She little knew the dilemma that my Grandma had.

La maquinita se descompuso,

The machine broke down,

y no había forma de arreglarla para aquel uso.

and there was no way to fix it in time.

-Y ahora qué voy a hacer?-

And now what do I have to do?

Penso para sí:

She thought to herself,

¡A mano el vestido tendré que coser!

I will have to sew the dress by hand!

Puntada a puntada, mi abuela cosía

Stitch by stitch my grandma sewed

y cada puntada perfecta salía.

And every stitch came out perfect.

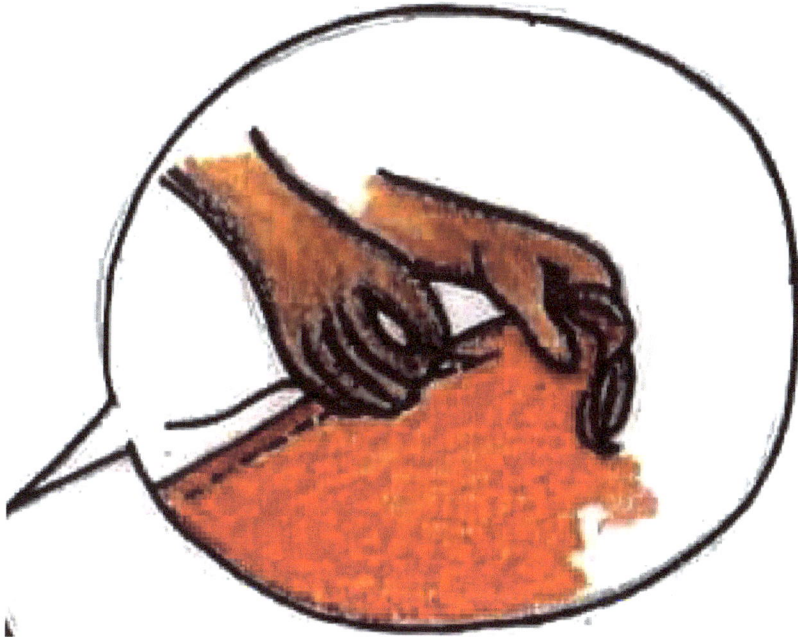

La clienta llegó,

The client arrived.

Mi abuela le explicó lo que le sucedió.

My grandma explained what happened.

Y esta se asombró

She could not believe

al ver aquellas puntadas tan perfectas que mi abuela cosió.

The perfect stitches my grandma sewed.

Mi abuela ¡Muy inteligente era!

My grandma was very smart!

www.ingramcontent.com/pod-product-compliance
Lightning Source LLC
Chambersburg PA
CBHW040035050426
42453CB00003B/123